Richard Grant White

Mr. Washington Adams in England

Richard Grant White

Mr. Washington Adams in England

ISBN/EAN: 9783744709804

Printed in Europe, USA, Canada, Australia, Japan

Cover: Foto ©ninafisch / pixelio.de

More available books at **www.hansebooks.com**

MR. WASHINGTON ADAMS
IN ENGLAND.

POCKET EDITIONS IN ONE SHILLING VOLUMES.

Authors' Editions.

MR. W. D. HOWELLS' WORKS

In Fourteen Volumes.

THE BREAKFAST TABLE SERIES

By Oliver Wendell Holmes

In Six Volumes.

RUDDER GRANGE.	WINTER SUNSHINE.
By Frank R. Stockton.	By John Burroughs.
ONE SUMMER.	OLD CREOLE DAYS.
By B. W. Howard.	By George W. Cable.

Others in preparation.

MR. WASHINGTON ADAMS IN ENGLAND

BY

RICHARD GRANT WHITE

AUTHOR OF
'ENGLAND WITHOUT AND WITHIN,'
ETC. ETC.

Author's Edition

EDINBURGH
DAVID DOUGLAS, CASTLE STREET
1883

Edinburgh University Press:
T. AND A. CONSTABLE, PRINTERS TO HER MAJESTY.

Frederic Ernest Allsopp.

I.

THE FELLOW-TRAVELLERS. OLD ENGLAND AND NEW ENGLAND.

ONE bright September day I was on my way from London to —— in ——shire, where I expected to ramble for half a week among the farmsteads and cottages, unknowing and unknown, and then to visit a gentleman of the county, whom I had not seen since he parted from me at my own door, leaving pleasant memories behind him. I was alone in the railway carriage, and was as nearly in a state of perfect happiness as a man could be who was away from home and from those who make it home, and the desire of whose life was not only unattained but unattempted. The air was soft; the greyblue sky was lightly clouded; the morning beamed with a mellow brightness that was like the smile of a happy woman. Sitting in the middle back seat, leaning at mine ease in mine inn, swift-moving, silent, secluded, luxurious, I looked alternately through one window and the other upon that beautiful human scenery of England which was such a never-ending, ever-varying source of delight to me that its only shadow was the regret which it now and then awakened that a certain steeple-crowned gentleman had not stayed at home and minded his business, instead of seeking that "freedom to worship God," which, having obtained, he immediately took vigorous measures to deny to others.

My reveries did not attain the

dignity of thought; and I was as nearly in the state of sweet-doing-nothing as is possible to a man of English blood and American birth in the nineteenth century. The speed of the train was diminished by almost insensible gradation, until we stopped at one of the minor way-stations, where I saw half a dozen persons waiting: a clergyman, manifestly, not only from the cut and colour of his coat, and his hat, and his white tie in the morning, but most of all from his very clerical but cheerful countenance; a roughish, sharp-eyed commercial traveller or two; a lean, pale, spinster-looking gentlewoman, with a maid of dangerous freshness of lip and roundness of waist, carrying her bag; and a farmer, not big and burly, but rather under-sized, with a gnarled and almost knotted visage. All these were evidently going short distances, and they disappeared into other carriages; when, just as the train was about moving, my open door was darkened by a porter who had in his hand a small portmanteau, on which I at once saw, among other labels and relics of others, two that interested me,—Boston and Roma. "Step quick, sir, please," said the porter; and the passenger was in his seat, with his portmanteau at his feet, before I recognised him. "Why, Humphreys, is it you? How came you here?" "In a fly," he answered, with a smile, partly at his old joke, partly of pleasant recognition. After a grasp of the hand, which was somewhat closer than it would have been if we had met in Broadway or in Beacon Street, we fell into the quick inquiring and replying chat of compatriots who meet unexpectedly in a strange country.

Mansfield Humphreys, whose first name was William, but who was always called by his second, that of his mother's family, was a New England man, who spent a great part of his time in New York. His people were of well-settled respectability in the interior of Massachusetts: his father, a judge, an Episcopalian when Episcopalians were rare in the Old Commonwealth, an unflinching Federalist in the waning days of Federalism; his mother, the daughter of a Congregational minister. They were one of those numerous New England families who, having lived savingly in the past on fewer hundreds a year than many of them now have thousands, had yet been known through generations for their culture, their fine breeding, and their character. Whether all the men were brave we know not; and if all the women were not virtuous, that too was never known; but they were of that order of New England folk among whom the doing of a shabby thing was almost social death;

and for generations they had held their heads high with modest dignity; so that in the times when representatives were chosen because they were thought to be worthy of consideration and the fittest men to speak and act for their fellow-citizens, the Humphreys sat again and again in the General Court of Massachusetts. He was a Harvard man, and a lawyer by profession; but he had appeared little in the courts, and was chiefly employed as counsel for railway companies, in one or two of which he was a shareholder.

In the civil war, after standing uncertain for a while (for he was no abolitionist), he became a very pronounced Unionist; not because he went with the multitude, but chiefly, I suspect, because of his resentment of the political domineering and social arrogance of the South. He did not go into the army; for although he was very young at the time, he thought he could do more service out of the field than in it. "I've no military instincts," he said; "if I were to put on a uniform, I should only feel as if I was going to a *bal costumé* in a character that didn't suit me. I hardly know one end of a gun from the other; I never in my life fired even a revolver; and in battle I should count only as one man, either to shoot or to be shot at; but of such perhaps if I stayed at home I might count for quite half a dozen." Wherefore he stayed; and he did count for many half-dozens by his energy and skill in affairs, and his indomitable spirit in the darkest days of the Union. He was very versatile; and one unexpected manifestation of a special talent brought us into close communion. In a series of amateur dramatic performances, got up for the purpose of combining social entertainment with the raising of funds for the equipment of a regiment, I had acted as a sort of stage manager, and he had been general business manager and treasurer; but on the defection of one of the principal amateur artists, and the despair of the company at finding a *remplaçant*, he, to the surprise of all, declared that he would take the vacant *rôle* himself. To the still greater surprise of all, this sober lawyer and then nascent railway manager, displayed a marked histrionic ability. Although he was a fine-looking fellow, he had a face and a figure that were not impressively individual, and when he appeared upon the stage he was dressed and made up with such skill that, if his name had not been known, his nearest friends would not have recognised him. He played with an entire unconsciousness of self, and with such a dry, pungent humour that his speeches told like rifle-bullets on his audience. His success did not turn his head. After the war was over, he could not be induced to repeat his theatrical performances. He subsided again into his business, and grew moderately rich ; and in the mature man who looked after stocks and legislatures no one, except a few who remembered the young fellow of fifteen years before, would have supposed there was an amateur actor of the first quality.

This was the man who dropped by my side, out of the clouds into a railway carriage. As we chatted, the train stopped again, and there entered our compartment a tall, fine-looking man, with dark eyes and hair, aquiline features, and military-looking moustache and whiskers in which a little grey was gleaming. He looked strong and alert, notwithstanding a pale face and a rather slender figure. Taking off his hat, after bidding us goodmorning, he put it into the rack above his head, and substituted for it a little black silk smoking-cap. Then he took up a railway novel and began to read.

Soon, turning to Humphreys, who was on the opposite seat, he said, "I beg your pahdon, but would you kindly tell me if this is a fast train? I forgot to inquire."

"With pleasure," said Humphreys; "but I don't know, myself. I'm quite a stranger here,—an American."

If instead of this answer in Humphrey's sweet, rich voice, he had received a snub, he could hardly have shown more astonishment in the change of the expression of his face. His eye rested a moment on Humphreys, and with "Ah, thanks," he slowly went back to his book. After reading a while, with an uneasy hitch or two of his elbows, he suddenly turned to Humphreys again, saying, " I beg your pahdon, but you said you were an American. You weren't jokin' ?"

"Not at all ;" and after a glance at me, with an affirmative glance in reply, "My friend here and I are both Americans,—Yankees. I've been here before, but I believe this is his first visit to England."

"Indeed! That's very surprisin'. Will you pahdon a stranger for saying so, but (I've never been in America) you're not at all the sort of person that we take Americans to be, and generally find 'em, if you'll excuse me for sayin' so. Indeed, I know I'm takin' a liberty; but I was so much surprised that—that—I'm sure—I hope you'll pahdon me."

It is impossible to exaggerate the manly courtesy and deference of his manner as he spoke, looking frankly and modestly from his hazel eyes, and the little hesitation in his speech rather lent it grace and charm.

" Pray don't apologise," said Humphreys, " but let me ask in turn, What sort of creature do you expect an American to be,—black, with woolly hair, or copper-coloured, with a scalp-lock and a tomahawk in hand ?"

He laughed gently, and replied, " Not exactly that ; at least except in some cases. But the few Americans that I've seen could be told for American across a theatre : their faces, their figures, their carriage, the cut of their clothes, all told it ; and if one were blind they could be known by their voices, and, if you'll pahdon me, by the very queer language they used, which was English merely because it wasn't anything else. I know I've no right to presume on these criticisms to you ; but you seemed to invite it, after kindly passin' over my first intrusion."

"Pray be at ease on that score. We're very glad, I'm sure, of a little enlightenment in regard to those very queer people, 'the Americans,' who you seem to think are all as like as Rosalind's halfpence. But now pardon me for saying, in my turn, that if you were to come to Boston, you would be taken, by most of my friends, at least in your evening dress, for a Yankee, except by those whose quick ears detected some slight John Bullish inflections in your voice, or whose quick eyes discovered some kindred and equally slight peculiarities of manner."

"I taken for a Yankee!" and he looked blank, and even slightly aghast.

It was the nearest approach to unpleasantness that our fellow-traveller had yet been guilty of; but it was so honest and simple, so plainly without thought of offence, and so earnest, that Humphreys and I enjoyed it and laughed; at which he blushed like a girl, and then laughed himself, with gleaming teeth and mobile lips.

"Why," said Humphreys, "are you not English?"

"What a question! To be sure I am."

"English for many generations?"

"For more than I know. My people were here when William the Conqueror came over."

"So were mine; so were my friend's; so were those of most of our friends at home. Did you ever think of that?"

"Ah—yes. Just so; quite so, quite so. That's an old story. But hasn't there been some admixture—ah, some interminglin', or—ah, somethin'? Else how could we tell an American the moment we look at him,—the very moment, don't you see? You find 'em in Paris, and all over the Continent, and you can tell 'em as you pass 'em in the street."

"Hardly, it would seem; for here's a case this morning, perhaps two," with a glance at me, who kept silence, "in which it seems the sure tests failed."

"Ah, yes,—'m; just so; quite so, quite so. You're right there. Bless my soul! I never was so astonished in my life as when you coolly told me you were an American."

"Coolly?"

"I beg your pahdon;" and again he blushed. "I meant no offence."

"Not more than I did, I'm sure, when I said that you might be taken for a Yankee."

I saw by his eye that he winced again, internally; but he said nothing.

"Of course," said Humphreys, in an easy, off-hand manner, "we can always tell an Englishman by his face and his figure, and his dress and his speech."

"Ah, just so; I should think so,"

with a little involuntary drawing of himself up.

"Oh, yes; we all know an Englishman by his being red-faced and bull-necked and clumsy, with coat and trousers of a furious check, and a waistcoat of a different suit, and a lot of chains and rings, and his saying Hengland for England, and calling a hen an N. We can't mistake them." And as Humphreys told this off, there was a good-natured smile upon his lip, and a twinkle in his eye that made it impossible for our carriage companion to take offence at what he himself had provoked. But he rejoined quickly and rather sharply, dropping his voice—

"I beg your pahdon, I beg your pahdon; you said that you'd been here before. Did you ever happen to be in the company of an English gentleman?"

"This morning, at least, I hope

and believe," said Humphreys, bowing, and looking him very steadily in the eye.

There was a slight pause, and then the Englishman said, "I ask your pahdon, I ask your pahdon; I see I was wrong. But it's all so very odd, so very strange. The truth is that— you see that, as I told you, I've never been in America, and the few Americans I've seen I've met by chance, and didn't know who or what they were,—and that, by the way, isn't an easy thing to find out about Americans; and so—well, I suppose," with a pleasant smile and a very sweet and simple courtesy,—"I suppose I haven't happened to fall in with an American gentleman until this morning."

"A Roland for my Oliver," said Humphreys, with a frank smile; "but let us leave compliments and fencing, and talk a little plain common-sense. What do you mean by an American?"

"Oh, a man born in America, to be sure,—a man from the States."

"That's a definition that would quickly land you on very queer and heterogeneous shores. For it would include some millions of negroes, some tens of thousands of Indians, to say nothing of a great number of sons of Irishmen and Germans, whose brothers and sisters, as well as whose parents, were born in Ireland or in Germany. Now all these people are almost as completely separated from each other, and from us Yankees, and from Virginians and South Carolinians, as if they or their parents had remained at home. The time will come when they—the whites among them at least—will all be blended into one people; but many generations must pass away before that is brought about. Meantime, they are all citizens of the United States, just as all your Irishmen and Scotchmen and

East Indiamen are British subjects. But although they are thus politically united, and being scattered over a half-continent that has no distinctive name, are called Americans for convenience' sake, because there is no other way of designating them, they are in no sense one people, like the English people, or the Irish, or the Scotch, or the French, or like the Germans and the Italians, who have been distinctive races or peoples from prehistoric times, but only recently have become politically nations."

"Ah, I see; just so, just so. But what has that to do with my taking you and your friend, as a matter of course, for Englishmen, and my being taken for—for—a Yankee?"

"Well, this: Are you not apt to forget that New England was settled by Englishmen who went over there in large numbers (nearly forty thousand in less than twenty years) two centuries and a half ago,—Englishmen who were, so to speak, the most English of their kind, typical representatives of the Anglo-Saxon race as it had been developed in England during one thousand years ; the men who beheaded Charles I. because he was a faithless tyrant, and who made the Commonwealth :—who, as John Richard Green has told you, were in great part men of the professional and middle classes ; some of them men of landed estate ; some clergymen, some London lawyers, or young Oxford scholars ; the bulk, god-fearing farmers ? Don't you forget that these men and their descendants, through a century and a half (with no important admixture), settled and built up the country, and framed a society and a system of government which, omitting only the elements of monarchy and aristocracy, was thoroughly English in its spirit, in its laws, and in its habits and customs—which indeed could not have been other than thoroughly English, because *they* were English; and that American Society, as they thus made it, was subjected to no considerable external influences until about fifty years ago? It is within that time, within the memory of men yet living and acting, that the emigration from other countries than England began. Fifty years ago the people of New England and Virginia (excluding the slaves) were probably the most thoroughly English people in the world."

The Englishman raised his eyebrows, and looked inquiringly.

"Because," Humphreys continued, in reply to the look, "there was less admixture of any foreign element among them than there was in England itself. You might then travel through New England in its length and breadth, and not encounter, in your journey, half a dozen names that were not English. Do you suppose that the blood, the nature, of these men was changed because, in contending for their rights as Englishmen, they had severed their political connection with the mother country? Did the absence of monarchy affect their race, or change their race traits? Were Cromwell's Ironsides any less Englishmen than Goring's troopers? Were Englishmen any less English under the Commonwealth than they had been before under Charles I., or than they became afterwards under Charles II.?"

"I suppose not. I never thought of that. But they were in England."

"And you suppose that that made them Englishmen? I thought, on the contrary, that Britain became England because Englishmen lived there, possessed the country, and ruled it."

"Very true. Just so; quite so, quite so."

"Well, if a large body of Englishmen went to another country, and possessed it and ruled it, would they therefore cease to be Englishmen?"

"N-n-no; I can't see exactly how they would. But they might change, you know, in time, and by intermixture with other people,—natives of the new country, the aborigines, you know; and that would modify their language and their customs, and so gradually make them a different people."

"So it might, in a long period of time. But what are two centuries in the life of a race, and above all a race so scrupulously averse to social intermixture as the English race is when it colonises? Aborigines! Why, the Englishmen that came from Jutland into Britain didn't sweep it so clean of the British tribes, as the Englishmen who came from Old England to America swept their part of the country clean of Americans. Yes" (in answer to a look of surprise at the word), "Americans; for you've only to turn back less than a hundred years in English literature to find the word 'American' applied (and rightly) only to the tribes for whose miserable remnants you have now to go to the Rocky Mountains, two thousand miles from Boston,—further than from London to St. Petersburg. And then these Englishmen clung with singular tenacity to every element of their English birthright, its laws, its language; and chiefly to its English Bible, which has been thus far the most indestructible of all the bonds of union between scattered men of English race, even the most godless of them. But we're getting into deep waters for a railway chat, and I'm almost lecturing you."

"No, no; do go on. I suppose I knew all this before; but I never saw it before quite in this light."

"Well, however it all may be that I've just been telling you, at the risk of being trite and commonplace, is it not reasonable in judging a country in which a new government and a new society have been established, to judge it by those who have been longest under the influences of the country, physical, political, and social? Must not they be the best examples of what that new country, as you call it, and that new government and society have produced?"

"Ah! 'm! seems so; can't say but they are."

"How could it be otherwise? Now the most thoroughly English-seeming men that you will find in America are New England men and Virginians whose families have been in New England and Virginia for two hundred years. I remember a man on shipboard whom not one of those whom you call Britishers "—

"We?"

"Surely you, or nobody. It is a word never heard in the United States: absolutely unknown except as a quizzical quotation of what you must pardon me for calling British blundering."

"Well, well!" said our railway friend, a little testily. "There would seem to be no end to our blunderin'. You mean, I suppose, your English shipmates."

"Some were English, yes; but some were Scotch, some Irish, and there was a handsome Welshman, with a sweet English wife. But they were all British subjects, as they might all have been citizens of the United States,—might they not?"

"I'm afraid you're an American Socrates, and are gettin' me into a corner with your questions; but I suppose that I must admit that they might."

"And in that case would they have ceased to be English, Irish, Scotch, and Welsh?"

"To be sure they would."

"How is that? Would the government under which they chose to live change their identity, their race, and make them other than they were born?"

"N-n-no. At least, I can't say just now how it would. But aren't you puttin' rather too fine a point on it, as we say in England?"

"And as we say in' New England. I think not. But be that as it may, this motley crowd of four races undertook to label some dozen or twenty of their fellow-passengers as foreigners, because they were born in America,—men of as unmitigated English blood as could be found between the Humber and the Channel.

But this one man whom I mentioned they positively refused to accept as an American, even upon the assurance of his countrymen; insisting upon it, in a hooting sort of way, that he was English. And so he was,— as English as King Alfred; but, as I happened to know, he was from the interior of New England, where his father's family and his mother's had lived for more than two hundred years."

"A singular exception, I suppose. There must always be such exceptions, you know."

"Pardon me, rather as *you* know; just such exceptions as you found my friend here and myself." And as Humphreys smiled, his good-natured colloquist smiled too, and said—

"You have me there. But you see, I'm no fair match for you. You have thought on this subject, and I haven't."

"And therefore you have undertaken to decide it; for yourself, at least."

"Come, come! This is getting to be a little too much. I didn't expect that when I asked a simple question I should be sat upon in this awful way;" saying this in the pleasantest tone and with perfect good-nature, and yet evidently feeling a little nettled at Humphrey's close pursuit.

"Isn't the truth of the matter that you—I mean you in the Old Home here—have done the sitting down yourselves for so long that you don't quite like any change in the fashion?"

There was a silence of a few moments, broken only by the half-musical hum with which a fast English railway train pursues its swift but gentle course; and I, looking out of the window, as we passed, upon a viaduct, over a pretty road, saw a great van toiling along just under us, and a humble foot-passenger resting himself on a bench under an old oak opposite a little inn, at the door of which stood a stout, red-faced woman, probably the wife of the publican. I had hardly had this characteristic glimpse of rural England, and we were whisking again through sprout-fields and meadows, when our companion resumed the conversation, saying, " Perhaps, perhaps. The truth is that likely enough we have been a little hard upon you, from Mrs. Trollope down."

"Ay," answered Humphreys; "you all begin with Mrs. Trollope's damnable book. And yet Mrs. Trollope was right."

" Right! And *you* say that !"

" I. So far as I have the means of knowing, Mrs. Trollope was quite correct in all her descriptions."

" Quite so," I said, putting in my

little oar for the first time, as the Englishman turned to me with an astonished and inquiring eye.

"And yet you called her book damnable."

"And so it was," said Humphreys; "professing as it did to give a picture of the domestic manners of the Americans, and taken, as it was, to be a correct representation of society in the United States. It was written in a pleasing and picturesque style,— for Mrs. Trollope's style was better than her son Anthony's; and that book has leavened, or rather soured and doughed, British opinion and tinged British feeling in regard to the Americans to this day."

"Correct, and yet damnable; pleasing and picturesque, and yet souring and doughing! Matters, I must say, are becoming rather complicated; 'mixed' I believe it's called in America."

"Do you know," said Humphreys, sharply, "anything of the geography of the United States, and did you ever hear of Botany Bay?"

"Oh, yes," replied our companion, blandly brightening; "I'm pretty well up there. I know, of course, that the States lie south of Canada, and north of the island of Nassau; and I know all about your big rivers and lakes, and your immense prairies, and the Rocky Mountains, and California, and all that sort of thing. But what has that to do with Botany Bay?"

"Do you know how far New Orleans and Cincinnati are from Boston and Philadelphia?"

"New Orleans? That's where the British troops lost a battle. Washington defeated us there, didn't he? You see I'm determined to be fair. Quite at the south, isn't it? And Cincinnatus,—one of your western towns isn't it, near Chicago? I suppose they must both be pretty well away from Boston; some two or three hundred miles or so."

"And do you know when Mrs. Trollope wrote her book?"

"I can answer that question of my American catechism too," he replied. "I know it's not a new book,— twenty or thirty years old; and since that time, I know," he continued, with a courtesy which I thought rather severely tried by Humphrey's sharp fire of questions, "the Americans have made great advances,— very great advances, indeed," bowing to both of us.

"My stars and garters! nothing of the sort," rejoined Humphreys, like a steel-trap. "If you mean that we've grown richer, and bigger, and stronger, very well; that's true enough. But if you mean that we've made great advances in morality, in social refinement, and particularly in domestic manners, to use Mrs. Trollope's very good phrase, permit me to assure you, you're quite wrong. This was before my memory: I'm not praising the doings of the days when I was a boy. I spare you the quotation "—

"*Sese puero,*" murmured our friend.

—"but if you will look into the books of some British travellers who preceded Mrs. Trollope a generation or so, you will find that they present a picture of morals and manners in the United States much more admirable than could be composed from the columns of our own newspapers at the present day."

"You have been deterioratin' then, you mean to say?"

"Looking at the surface of our society without discrimination, it must be admitted that the deterioration has been great in those respects."

"I'm sorry to hear it; and to tell

you the truth, I think somethin' of the same sort has been goin' on in England. To what do you attribute it?"

"Several causes; but chiefly, our great and sudden increase in wealth, the war, and—largely, European influence."

"Whew!"—a very soft whistle of surprise.

"Not such European influence as would be likely to be under your personal cognisance, or to occur to you in your estimate of social forces. But let me go on as I began. The deterioration in morals is so certain and so well known that no one thinks of disputing it. To look through a file of one of our leading newspapers for the last fifteen years is to be led to the conclusion that personal honesty has become the rarest of virtues in the United States, except public probity, which seems no longer to exist.

The very ruins of it have disappeared. Our State legislatures, instead of being composed of men to whom their constituents looked up, are now composed of men upon whom their constituents look down,—not second-rate, nor even third-rate, but fourth and fifth rate men, sordid in morals and vulgar in manners, who do politics as a business, for the mere purpose of filling their own pockets. No one thinks of disputing this more than the presence of the blood-sucking insects of summer. Congress itself is openly declared by our own journals to be, because it is known to be, the most corrupt body in civilised Christendom. Within the last fifteen years we have seen men occupying the highest, the two very highest, positions in the government of the United States, who were not only purchasable, but who had been purchased, and at a very small price. I know what I say, and mean it" (in answer to a look of surprise). "The Cabinets, during the same period, have been so rotten with corruption that the presence in them of two or three men of integrity could not save them. Worse even than this, judges are openly called Mr. This-one's judge, or Mr. That-one's; their owner being generally the controlling stockholder and manager of some great corporation, which coins wealth for him and his satellites by schemes of gigantic extortion. I know something of this by personal observation. There was a time when the bench of the United States was not inferior in probity, and hardly in learning or ability, to that of Great Britain. As to manners, did you see that social sketch in Punch ticketed "In Mid-Atlantic," in which a bishop or a dean, who has plainly been engaged in an upper-deck fair-day chat with an American mother, turns to her son, a lad in knickerbockers, and looking with benign reproof upon him, says, ' My young friend, when I was of your age it was not thought decorous for young people to mingle in the conversations of their elders, unless they were requested to do so.' And young Hopeful replies, 'That must have been eighty years ago, and we've changed all that now.' The cut is hardly an exaggeration ; but here are my friend and myself, who are little more than half the age attributed to your bishop, and who can tell you that in our boyhood that point of breeding was not only taught and insisted on, but punctiliously observed among all respectable New England folk. And who, at that time, among such people, even not in our boyhood, would have ventured to come up to two persons engaged in conversation, and break directly in upon them with another topic, at his pleasure, or for his interest, as now is done constantly? Deterioration of manners indeed!"

"But these are comparatively triflin' matters, mere surface marks,— not peculiar to America, you may be sure. Boys are saucier in England than they used to be; and here rude men thrust themselves upon you now with a freedom that certainly shows the world is movin'; but as to which way, they and you might have a different opinion."

"Surface marks! So are the bubbles on a stream; but they float with its current, and the foul air that fills them comes from the bottom. Let me tell you, *ex cathedrâ*, what I know, merely as every observing man who has the means of knowing knows: that the manners and the manner, as well as the morals, of America—let us say of Boston and Philadelphia, for example, and the surrounding country —were of a much finer type in the days of our fathers than they are in ours. Behaviour is common now in splendid drawing-rooms, filled with every attainable object of luxury and of taste, which then would not have been tolerated in modest parlours of people who lived frugally and worked hard for their moderate incomes. Among them, young people did not lounge and loll about and talk slang in the presence of their elders and of ladies."

"Come, come! Aren't you playin' the middle-aged cynic? That's not at all peculiar to America. The very same change has been remarked upon here."

"And therefore," remarked Humphreys, with a little smile, " Americans have been becoming *un*like Englishmen? Strange, that among people so unlike, the social changes should have been the same within the same period of time!"

"H'm! Democratic tendencies; influence of democracy in both countries; lack of deference for authority in both countries."

"Perhaps. But among the changes in manners in England haven't you observed the incoming of a certain mildness and gentleness of tone, a considerate charity for weakness and misfortune, and for the feelings of inferiors? Are personal defects and failings, and the ridicule that Juvenal tells us is inherent in poverty, now openly made the butts of the more fortunate so much as they used to be, say, even when Miss Austen wrote her novels?"

"No, they're not. In that respect I must say there has been a marked improvement. I suppose the same has taken place with you."

"No."

"No?"

"Not at all: simply because it was

not needed. I don't know how it was at the South ; but among New England people of decent breeding in colonial days, and in the early years of the republic, any reflection upon personal defects or misfortune, any assumption of superiority because of mere money prosperity, was regarded as the most offensive form of ill-manners ; so much so, that among such people it may be said to have been almost unknown. And this social trait may be taken as typical of the tone and the manners of New England society at the time we are speaking of."

" Very admirable, if—pahdon me— you 're sure you 're correct ; and quite destructive to a suggestion I was about to make,—that the Americans, whose manners and mental tone and habits you seem to think should be taken as characteristic, are not real Americans, products of your soil, but Europeanised Americans."

"Now," said Humphreys, smartly, "if you use that phrase and take that position, I shall—to adopt an expression of the elegant Miss Harriet Byron's—'rear up.' The Americans of whom I am speaking are, true enough, not products of the soil;—in the name of Christopher Columbus how could they be?—but they were those who had been free from European influence, not only from their birth, but for generations,—people who had never been in Europe, and whose forefathers had never been there from the time when they first went to America, two hundred and fifty years ago. *They* were the people who, Lord Lovelace said, in Queen Anne's time, had, with their colonial and republican simplicity of life, the manners of courtiers, and wondered (ignorant as he was) where they could have got their breeding. He reminds me of another more distinguished peer, or man who became a peer,—Bulwer, Lord Lytton. Once, at his own table, when there was a discussion as to some matter of taste as to which an American, there present, ventured to express an opinion adverse to that prevalent in England, and to refer to the standard in his own country, Bulwer said, turning pointedly to him, 'We're not accustomed to look to America for opinions on matters of good taste,'—a speech which would have been regarded as very rude in America, even in the rural districts of New England ; above all, to a guest at one's own table."

" Rather rough, I must confess. But you mustn't judge all English gentlemen by that; for, with all his fine talk, I'm inclined to think that Bulwer was somethin' of a sham."

" I'm not surprised to hear you say so ; and I don't judge all English gentlemen by such a speech,—only some of them ; but unfortunately they are they whose voices are most frequently heard by Americans."

"Ah, yes; just so, just so; just as the American voices that we most frequently hear are pitched in a tone not quite so agreeable as—those I've heard this morning. Pahdon me for being a little personal."

"With all my heart, so far as your intention goes; but as to the fact, I don't know that your apology much helps the matter. For, excuse me for saying that your very apology shows either that you speak in ignorance, or that you pick out what is antipathetic to you, and label that, and that only, as American. Your countrymen, even the intelligent and kindly intentioned, are so stung with a craze after something peculiarly American from America that they refuse to accept anything as American that is not extravagant and grotesque. Even in literature they accept as American only that which is as strange and really as foreign to the taste and habits of the most thoroughbred Americans as it is to them."

" Bret Harte ?"

" Verily: I should say so. The personages in Bret Harte's brilliant sketches are just as strange, and in the same way strange, to decent people in Boston and Philadelphia as they are to people in London and in Oxford; and they interest the one exactly as they do the other, and for the same reasons: and they have no peculiarly American character."

" That's an astonishin' criticism."

" None but that given them by their scenes being laid in a part of America three thousand five hundred miles from Boston, farther in distance than from New York to London, and thrice as far in time. Any writer of Bret Harte's talent, whose mother tongue was English, would—must—have made them just as American as he did. And besides, the men he wrote about were no more American than British. Half the early Californian mining population were of British birth,—English or Scotch, with a few Irish."

"Are you sure of that?"

"Sure; if you don't pin me down to tens in a row of figures. Don't you remember in the letter of the Fifth Avenue belle to her California lover—

> 'And how I went down the middle
> With the man that shot Sandy McGee'?

And don't you remember that she herself was ould Follinsbee's daughter? Mr. McGee and Mr. Follinsbee were typical men, in whom your interest was as great as ours, and for whom your responsibility was much greater. But to turn back to Bulwer, and his pretty speech: he deserved, I hope you'll think, to have the truth told him,—that among Americans of the best breeding his earlier novels were condemned, although they were read."

" Ah, yes; for their immorality, I suppose. I've always heard that in such matters you were of a most exemplary particularity; although you seem, in those also " (with a sly smile) " to have made some progress."

" Less on that account than for their bad taste and their low social tone. Men of my age can remember hearing Bulwer spoken of in our boyhood, by our elders, as essentially vulgar, a snob,—a gilded snob, but none the less a snob. Is not that true?" turning to me.

"Yes," I answered; "but he improved in this respect astonishingly. There are few more remarkable phenomena in literature than Bulwer's moral growth. You would hardly believe that the same soul and the same breeding were in the man who wrote *Pelham* and *The Caxtons.*"

"But after all," urged Humphreys, "wasn't this the result rather of an intellectual perception of moral beauty than of a regenerate condition? Had he in him, the man who wrote *Pelham*, the capacity of ever becoming, at heart, a gentleman?"

"I'm afraid you're right," said our friend; "but haven't we taken rather a flyer? What has all this to do with Mrs. Trollope, and New Orleans, and Cincinnatus, and Botany Bay?"

"This," answered Humphreys, with a mild conclusive fall of his voice; "the people who thus condemned Bulwer, just as you condemn him, on the score of taste and true good breeding, were the very Americans whose domestic manners Mrs. Trollope's book misrepresented."

"Beg pahdon, I thought you said her book was true."

"So it was. It did not caricature, —or very little. What it did was to present to the ignorant and prejudiced people of England a carefully made, but lively and graphic, series of sketches of society, which were about as fair representations of the domestic manners of such Americans I ever met under a roof as a series of like sketches of the society of Botany Bay at that time would have been of any English people that you are likely to know anything about."

"I don't quite understand. Pray explain."

"Mrs. Trollope published her book not twenty or thirty years ago, but fifty. She entered the America which she professed to describe, not at Boston, New York, or Philadelphia, but at New Orleans; and going up the Mississippi a thousand miles,— yes" (in answer to a look of astonished inquiry), "one thousand miles, and more,—she established herself as the keeper of a sort of big milliner's shop, or bazaar, at Cincinnati. Now Cincinnati is not two or three hundred miles from Boston or Philadelphia, but almost a thousand; and it's not near Chicago, but three hundred miles from it; and when she was there Chicago didn't exist. Cincinnati was then not only its thousand miles from Boston and Philadelphia, but as socially remote from any of the centres of civilisation in which the domestic manners of the Americans could be properly studied as Botany Bay was from London and Oxford."

Doubt, astonishment, and interest were strongly expressed in the face of our fellow-traveller; and he said, in a low apologetic tone, " But Botany Bay was a penal colony."

" Of course," said Humphreys, " I don't mean to compare the two places in that respect. They had no such likeness, even at that time. I specified Botany Bay only for the sake of using a name that would bring to your mind vividly a very remote colony of Englishmen cut off from intercourse with established English society, surrounded by a wild country, and composed chiefly of people whom circumstances had made pioneers on the remotest confines of civilisation. You in England have to reach your colonies of that sort by sea; we, so vast is the territory of the United States, reach ours by land. The country around Cincinnati then, within a few miles, was covered by the primeval forest, through which people who must travel passed upon tracks rather than roads, on horseback or in vehicles of the rudest and most primitive construction. It was then the far West, and not only physically distant, but a great deal farther removed from the long-established and slowly-developed social centres of America than any place in the world is now from any other place, except the interior of Russia, Siberia, and Southern Africa. My father had to go to Ohio, at that time or later, on some professional business connected with a land claim. He used to tell the story of it years afterward; and child as I was, I shall never forget his description of his experiences: how he was two weeks in getting there, creeping across the State of New York in a canal boat, travelling through Ohio on horseback, with saddle-bags, his papers in one and his few toilet articles in another, and his scanty wardrobe in a leathern valise strapped behind his saddle—I have it yet:— his description of the queer, uncouth people that he met, the privations he endured: how one day, when he had ridden from morning almost till night without coming upon anything like an inn, he stopped at a house that seemed to consist of two or three rooms, and asked for something to eat; and how the mistress of the establishment, who was the only person visible, set before him a coarse earthen dish, in which were some slices of cold boiled pork surrounded by dirty congealed fat, some half-sodden cakes of Indian corn, and a jug of whisky; and how the repulsiveness of the viands and of all the surroundings, including the slatternly woman, so affected him that, fatigued and famished as he was, he could not eat. For it's *à propos* of our subject for me to say, after some acquaintance with society in England and on the Continent, that he was one of the daintiest and most fastidious of men, although his father had reared his family with difficulty upon a slender income. I remember that in his story this woman spoke of her husband as the Judge, or rather the Jedge."

" Judge!"

"Yes, he was a justice of the peace."

"A justice of the peace! Pahdon my repeatin' your words."

"You are surprised: naturally. Your justices of the peace are county gentlemen and clergymen. With us a justice of the peace is the very lowest in consideration of all official dignities, simply because it is the least profitable."

"This is very strange,—a justice of the peace holdin' his office for profit!"

"Yes; that is one of the differences between the two countries. And you may set this down as an axiom of general application : that everything in America is done, every position is sought, with a single eye to pecuniary profit."

"And have you no gentlemen of leisure and character who might hold such an important position?"

"Very few; and they don't want it. Why should they? It would bring them no distinction, no honour among men of their own condition in life, and would subject them to experiences from which they would shrink. We have some men of wealth who, to become senator, with a chance for the presidency or a first-rate foreign mission, will spend a moderate fortune."

" Bless my soul ! How, pray ? "

" In bribery : bribing caucus managers, bribing legislators, bribing even political parties ; and so establishing what in our politics are called claims. But we are wandering. It was in such society as she found in these then remote and uncivilised regions, and others little differing from them, that Mrs. Trollope drew her pictures in all her books about the States, and labelled them *Domestic Manners of the Americans*. She has at the end of her book a few pages of kind approval of Boston, New York, and Philadelphia.

Why, I can remember that our friends used to listen to my father's descriptions of his Western travel as they would now if a man had returned from Patagonia or Japan; quite ignorant that pictures of that strange life were accepted by the world of Europe as faithful descriptions of *their* manners and customs. The great difficulty with you here upon this subject is that to you America—you don't know exactly what the name means, and indeed it is very vague and meaningless—is simply America, all one and the same; and that Americans are simply Americans, all alike. At the present day they are becoming more and more alike, under the shaping material and moral forces, which have been developed during the last twenty years; but before that limit of time the unlikeness was greater than you seem to be able to imagine."

"Quite so, I should say, from what

you tell me of the effect of the strangeness upon yourselves."

"Strangeness, indeed! Let me tell you a little characteristic story of old New England domestic manners, which you may compare with your recollections of Mrs. Trollope's book. My friend here will assure you of its literal truth; for he knows it. In 1789, when Washington was travelling slowly through New England, receiving and paying visits, he called at a house in Connecticut, the master of which, although one of the leading men in his neighbourhood, a scholar, and one who lived comfortably, never saw one thousand dollars in money (that's two hundred pounds, you know) in a year in all his life. Washington, when he departed, was conducted to the door by his host and hostess, accompanied by their daughter, a young girl just in her 'teens. She of course did not presume to say good-bye to General Washington; but as she opened the door for him and stood modestly aside that he might pass out, the great ex-commander-in-chief of the ragged Continental army, looking down upon her from his six feet two of stature, and from his Olympian top of grandeur, laid his hand with stately kindness upon her head, saying, 'Thank you, my little lady; I wish you a better office.' 'Yes, sir,' she replied, doing reverence with a gentle curtsey, ' to let you in.'"

"By George! worthy of a duchess! Only half of 'em wouldn't be up to it. 'Twould take Waldegrave to say that."

"I shan't say it wasn't; but I know it is merely a somewhat salient and striking example of New England manners until within the last forty years or so; and among people who were without servants that opened their doors for them on any occasion."

"Most extrawd'nary condition of society!"

"Extraordinary to you, but quite natural to us at that time: the union of culture and character and fine manners with the absence even of moderate wealth was quite as common in New England as their union with wealth is here. Now the great mistake that you all make, in your uneasy search after 'the real American' and the American thing, is that you don't look for them among those who have made America what it is (or what it was till within the last few years), and who are the product of generations of American breeding, but among"—

Here the train slowed, and our fellow-traveller, interrupting Humphreys hurriedly, said, "This has been very interestin' to me; but now

I'm afraid I must say good-mornin'. Can't I have the pleasure of seein' you again, and your friend? See; this is my address," taking out his card, and writing a word or two on it in pencil. "If you're in my country, do look me up. Almost any one'll tell you where I live; and I'll be delighted to see you, gentlemen, both of you, and make you as comfortable as I can. Give you some good shoootin', too, as you'll come after the 1st."[1]

We exchanged cards, and parted pleasantly.

"Hi!" said Humphreys (showing

---

[1] It is only by the use of a superfluous *o* that I can indicate the prolonged vowel sound in this word, which is one of the very few and slight differences in pronunciation between English and New England or New York men of similar breeding. The dropping of the *g* from the syllable *ing* is not universal among men of this class in England, but it is very common; much more common than in the class just below them.

me the card, on which appeared in plain, bold script, every letter of which proclaimed Strongi'tharm—EARL OF TOPPINGHAM, and in pencil *The Priory, Toppington*), "I've a letter to him in my pocket from Dr. Tooptoe, his old tutor at Oxford, who says he's one of the best fellows in the world, but too independent; that is, from old Dr. Tooptoe's point of view. You may think it queer that he asked two strangers, that he chanced upon in a railway carriage, to his house. With us, we should never venture on such a step; but here a man like him can do almost anything in reason without risk,—not only because of his rank, but because he's a tip-top man among his peers. And then we're Americans. If we were John Bulls, catch him at it! Besides, Americans are always interesting subjects of study, and objects to be exhibited."

"You know something of him, then.

He seems, indeed, a thorough good fellow, with charming manners."

"Only in a general way, and from what Dr. Tooptoe told me. Just think of it! that man took a double first class; and to do that at Oxford an Earl must work like any other man; besides, he counts for something in the House of Lords. And yet his ignorance! New Orleans was to him a place where the British troops were defeated, and by Washington! and the States lie to the north of the island of Nassau!"

"Well, well, what occasion has he had to know more? If he had, he could learn it all, pretty well, in an hour's smart reading."

"All the more! Why the deuce, then, doesn't he read, and waste an hour upon such a country as the United States, and where so many of his kindred are? Confound him! he thinks much of himself, as well he may, because his forefathers were at Toppington when William came over. So were mine, or very near by; and until the time of Henry VIII. they were both in very much the same rank of life. Then his ancestor was knighted, and soon got the Priory out of Cromwell, and then a peerage out of the king; and they went on marrying money and rising in rank, till since Walpole's time they 've been Earls."

"You 'll go, of course,—with your letter and his invitation, too?"

"H'm, I am not so sure of that. Where are you going now?"

"After knocking about a few days, as I told you, I shall go to Boreham Hall. Sir Charles has asked me there to spend two or three days."

"Boreham Hall! You 'll find it dreadfully dull there."

"Why? Sir Charles was pleasant enough when he was in New York."

"He was well enough ten years

ago; good-natured, and a gentleman, and all that. But he has married, since, a brewer's daughter, who brought him fifty thousand pounds, and who is as tame as a sheep, and bleats just like one; and he's settled down into a mere squire, and has grown burly and squirish. But that'll do very well. You're sure to go to Lord Toppingham's. All these people know each other, and all about each other; that's one comfort of their society. Borcham Hall is only a few miles from Toppington Priory,—just a pleasant ride, or walk; and you're sure to go if you will. It suits me well."

"How?"

"Why, you see these people are so beset with their craze after their real Americans that I've a notion to give my Lord Toppingham an opportunity of seeing one. In your few days of knocking about, I can find one Washington Adams, who's over here,

I believe, and who's just the sort of man for the purpose. I'll send Dr. Tooptoe's letter to Toppington Priory, enclosed in one saying I'm prevented from coming myself for the present, but that I shall take the liberty of introducing a friend, a real American. Yes," with a brightening eye, "by Jove, I'll do it!"

"Rather a cool proceeding, under the circumstances."

"Oh, it'll do,—under the circumstances, as you say,—especially if you're there at the time. I know my man. So when you're going to the Priory just drop me a line at B——, and it'll be all right."

"But who is Washington Adams?"

"Don't you know Washington Adams, the Honourable Washington J. Adams, Wash Jack Adams, as they call him? Why, he's the Member of Assembly from your own district."

"Quite likely; but I don't know him."

"That argues yourself unknown, as I once heard an editor say to him, with a sober face;—and to see him expand and beam with credulous vanity! He's the son of old Phelim McAdam, who ran two gin-mills in Mackerelville,[1] and who instead of dying in the odour of drunkenness, as you'd suppose, hardly ever was drunk in his life; he might have been a drunker and a better man; he made some money by his gin-mills, set up respectability, and joined the Republican party."

"An Irishman in New York join the Republican party!"

"Irishman yourself! as he would have said. Mr. Phelim McAdam was

[1] A part of New York corresponding to the Seven Dials in London. The name, given in derision, has no significance, and is merely fantastic.

an American born. Never was such a flagrant example of Americanism. Thus it was," in answer to my look of wonder: "Phelim McAdam was the son of an Irish emigrant. He came near being born in no country, but under the British flag; for his mother was expecting his appearance on the voyage, as she approached the shores of the home of the free and the land of the brave. But the lady lagged, or the good ship hastened, and Phelim first saw the light of freedom dimmed by filtering through the dirty panes of the upper windows of a Mackerelville tenement house, and bloomed upon the world a true-born American, whatever that may be. His gin-mills brought him some money, as I said before, and he married the daughter of a Division Street pawnbroker, who came out of —the Lord knows where!—but who was sharp and smart and ambitious;

and at her instigation he cut his Irish connection, moved up town, dropped the M^c from his name, and signed himself 'P. Adam,' to which the lady, who ere long set up a visiting card, quietly added an *s*. And so, in ten or fifteen years,—you know fifteen years is the beginning of all things in New York,—no one recognised, in a paragraph mentioning, to the lady's delight, 'P. Adams, Esq., of East Eleventh Street,' the 'McAdam, Phelim, liquors, Essex Street,' of the New York directory."

"You seem strangely well-informed on such a subject."

"You forget that I've been a railway lawyer, and am familiar with the lobby. He bought some shares in one, and, aided by his wife, got upon the Board."

"His wife?"

"She was a handsome hussy, scheming and pushing, and as crafty as

Satan ; and one winter she went to Albany, where I saw her, and had occasion to find out all about her,— all that was find-out-able. This was long ago; during the civil war. Well, as I was saying, like most of his sort, he was exceedingly American ; and oh, it was edifying to hear him, with an upper lip that weighed a pound, and a nose like a perforated pimple, talk about 'them low Irish.' Consequent upon his American pride, his son—the only one with which his 'lady' condescended to favour him —was borne away from the font with the name Washington Jackson Adams; which, when he went into politics— as he did soon after reaching his majority—was trimmed, in that elegant style which is distinctive of New York politics, into Wash Jack Adams ; often it became Washed Adams ; and this, after a certain investigation, the democratic *Penny*

Trumpet converted into Whitewashed Adams,—a name that might have been fastened upon him if he had been important enough to be talked about. Now, he's just the sort of creature that our friends here recognise as a real American; he's decent-looking enough,—not at all Irish; took after his mother; and I've a notion of giving some of them a chance to see him. So, good-bye! Don't forget to let me know." This passed as we neared his station. He and his portmanteau disappeared; but just as the train was starting he came rushing back, and looking in said, "You've never seen this Washington Adams?"

"Not I."

"Well, if it should occur to you that you ever did at any time, keep quiet."

"As a pretty widow about her age." And on I went toward Boreham.

II.

BOREHAM HALL.
SOCIETY IN AMERICA.

II.

BOREHAM HALL. SOCIETY IN AMERICA.

BOREHAM was one of those country-houses, found here and there in England, which in their time have served many uses. Its oldest part consisted of a small, low, square tower, built of flint and rubble, in which a mixture of red tiles seemed to indicate that it stood upon the site of a yet older structure, of Roman origin. Another part, in fine old brickwork, was shown to have been once a religious house, by the cross fleury upon its gable and the abbot's mitre over the principal door. It had not improbably been an outlying grange of the great priory at Toppington. To these had been added, in the latter part of Elizabeth's reign, a long, two-story, beam-and-plaster edifice, which contained, among other rooms, the drawing-room, a library, and a dining-room; the last bossed and gnarled with heavy oak carving, and having a great bay-window, large enough to hold a dinner-table and the chairs and guests and servants of a goodly dinner-party. This window looked out upon an old moat, which had evidently some connection with the little tower, and which, now dry and covered with beautiful green sward, was still crossed by a bridge or causeway, over which the great drive through the park led up to the principal entrance, which was in the Elizabethan part of the house. An opposite window, twice as broad as it was high, looked out upon a square court, paved with round stones, three sides of which were formed by the house, and the fourth by a wall, in which was a door leading to the stables. The stone pavement of the court was pierced by two yew-trees, which cast a gloomy shadow through the inner windows, and over a gallery on which the doors and windows of the upper rooms of the Elizabethan part of the house opened.

Having written to Sir Charles that I should reach the nearest station by a certain train, I found his carriage there, and was driven across the moat about five o'clock in the afternoon. My host met me in the hall, and gave me a quiet and undemonstrative welcome, which, however, I saw and felt was a hearty one. After a brief visit to my room, I went to Lady Boreham's parlour, where she was about dispensing afternoon tea. As I entered the room it impressed me with a sense of gloomy respectability. It was richly and comfortably furnished; but although it was, and was called, " Lady Boreham's parlour," nothing in it told of the grace and charm of a woman's presence.

My hostess received me with a sad propriety of demeanour which was somewhat depressing, but which I found was her general manner to all persons, whatever their rank, from peers and peeresses down to her own servants. As to herself, her face was pallid and of a pasty complexion; her hair, a toneless brown, and twisted at the front into some stiff curls, that stood like palisades before a queer little cap; her eyes, a dull grey; her nose, quite shapeless; and from her always half-open mouth there projected slightly two large white teeth. She was not bony, nor even slender; yet a mannish absence of roundness and fulness deprived her figure of all the grace and charm peculiar to womanhood. What she lacked in this respect, however, appeared in some excess in Sir Charles. He had, truly, changed in ten years. He was quite two stone heavier; the bloom that I had admired so much on his cheek had deepened in tint and thickened in quality; although he was not yet forty, his hair was thinning rapidly on the top of his head; and his manner had become as heavy as his person. Indeed, I found, during my brief visit, that for him life was made up of looking after his estate, hunting, shooting, reading the London *Times*. and dinner, last, not least. He did not read *The Saturday Review* or *The Spectator;* but Lady Boreham hungrily gloated upon *The World*, of which I never saw him take any notice, except by once tossing it contemptuously out of his way.

Three other guests at Boreham hardly require mention. One, a younger sister of my hostess, was almost her mere duplicate: two and three were a Mr. Grimstone and his wife, as to whom I could only discover that he was a Member of Parliament and of the Carlton Club, and that she was apparently without an idea or an emotion not connected with the *Court Circular*. The ladies were entirely devoid of personal attraction, and their toilets on all occasions were distressing. How these people managed to live through that part of each successive twenty-four hours during which they were not eating and sleeping was a mystery. They rarely exchanged a word that was not required by the ordinary civilities of social life, as to which they were unexceptionably and somewhat consciously correct and proper. And yet there was an air of solid respectability and good faith about them which, although their society was wholly without charm, even to each other, had a value that received a constant silent expression. One felt that they were very safe people to meet in any relation of life.

There were, of course, the customary attendants of a great house in England. One of these, Lady Boreham's own maid, whom I saw on two or three occasions, was one of the most beautiful women I ever encountered. I could not look at her without thinking of a June rose. Her noble figure was just tall enough to be a little distinguished, and she carried her finely poised head with such an air that her little cap became a coronet of beauty's nobility. Her manners were quite as good as Lady Boreham's; and her manner was as superior as that of the so-called Venus of Milo might be to that of the Venus of a burlesque. But if she had been some sort of attendant clockwork machine in petticoats, her mistress could not have treated her with less apparent recognition of a common humanity. Indeed, I do verily believe that Lady Boreham was quite unconscious that here was a woman constantly about her who, whenever she appeared, blotted her mistress out of existence for any man who had eyes and a brain behind them. The one fact ever present to her consciousness, as I discovered, was that she was Lady Boreham, and had brought her husband fifty thousand pounds; with which price she seemed to think that she had bought a throne and an allegiance from which she could never be cast out. And she had, so far as her husband and her guests were concerned. I must give them the credit of being, or seeming, as indifferent to "Wilkins"—the beauty's name—as she was herself. Wilkins was a "young person" who performed certain needful offices in an acceptable manner. It was well that Sir Charles was not a man of finer perceptions and a more flexible nature.

Lady Boreham was, however, not without curiosity; and on my second day at the Hall she led me to talk about society in America, as to which her notions seemed somewhat less correct and clear than those of a Vassar College[1] girl might be about Abyssinian court etiquette. "Did American women like being spiritual wives? What was a spiritual wife? If Brigham Young took the hustin's to be President, would all the women vote for him? Would all his wives vote for him? What could he do with them if they didn't? How many wives had he? Weren't most Americans Mormons, or Spiritualists,

---

[1] At Poughkeepsie, on the Hudson : founded by an English brewer who grew rich there : the typical *officina* of sweet girl graduates.

or somethin'? Was it true that American women could get a divorce whenever they liked? And *was* it true—with a furtive glance at the window where Maud sat netting—that in America a man might marry his deceased wife's sister? Did all Americans live at 'otels? And did American women come down to breakfast in full dress and di'mon's?"

The temptation was sore to give to these and like questions the replies which my hostess would have been pleased to receive; but I refrained myself, and told her the simple truth, to her astonishment and hardly concealed disappointment. The point as to which I had most difficulty in making my explanations understood was the difference of the laws in the several States as to marriage and divorce. Lady Boreham could not have been— was not, I found—ignorant of the difficulties that might arise in England because of Scotch marriages and Irish marriages; and yet she could not well apprehend that a woman might be legally married in Connecticut, and yet her marriage be at least disputable in New York, and that a divorce would be granted in Indiana upon grounds which would not be sufficient in New Jersey. To her, as to most of her sort in England, "the States" were "America," and America was governed by the President and Congress: the former, a kind of political Pope; the latter, a general legislative body, with the omnipotence of Parliament.

As I was explaining to her that Congress had to all intents and purposes no power over the individual lives and the personal relations of citizens of the United States; and that even murder, unless committed on the high seas, or in a fort or national vessel, was a crime, not against the laws of the United States, but against those of an individual State; and that debts were contracted under State laws, so that even the Supreme Court, the most important and powerful tribunal in the country, had no jurisdiction over them, except in certain specific cases,—the Member of Parliament, who was in the room, now reading a big Blue-book, now listening, pricked up his ears, and said—

"Yes; and your Supreme Court has made a nice mess of your national credit two or three times; sustaining American repudiation of debts,—refusing to pay money lent in good faith by British capitalists. Not very wise, permit me to say, thus to make repudiation a national characteristic, supported by your highest tribunal."

"I beg your pardon," I replied, "but perhaps you know that the United States Government has incurred rather a large indebtedness during the last twenty years. Will you kindly inform me if you know of the repudiation of any part of this debt?"

"Well, no—no; not at all, not at all; quite the contrary, I must admit. That debt was something quite awful; and it's been acknowledged and put in course of liquidation in a manner that—that—why, nobody expected anything of the sort."

"And why not, sir? let me ask. Why was it not expected? Has the United States Government been in the habit of repudiating its debts?"

"Well, no—no; not exactly the Government of the United States, I believe; but Pennsylvania, and Tennessee, and Virginia. They're in America, aren't they?"

"I've heard that Turkey has also failed to pay British creditors. Why have you not applied to the Supreme Court of the United States to compel the Turks to pay the interest and principal of their bonds?"

"Bless my soul, sir, your Supreme Court has no jurisdiction in Turkey! You haven't quite annexed the Sultan and his dominions, yet. You're joking; setting up for an American humorist."

"Not at all. I shouldn't presume to attempt so high a flight. Never was more serious in my life. Without going into particulars, I venture to say that in every case which you could have had in mind the Supreme Court merely decided the question of its own jurisdiction; and I venture also to suggest that if British capitalists would not be so blinded by the hope of getting six or seven per cent., instead of three, as to neglect making those inquiries as to the ability of borrowers in foreign countries, and as to the means of redress in default of payment, which they make at home, it would be wiser and more business-like; although I must admit

that such a course might be open to
the objection of involving some little
study of so trifling and disagreeable a
subject as the political structure and
internal polity of the United States."
And after a moment of silence I
turned again to the ladies.

"Now do tell us," said the M.P.'s
wife, "how you manage society in
America. I suppose you don't manage
it at all. How could you? You've
no Court, no peerage, no county
families. I suppose everybody goes
everywhere, and visits everybody else,
if they like. It must be amusin', in
a certain way; but do you find it
agreeable?"

My reply it is not necessary to re-
port in detail; and when the ladies
had gathered from it that, notwithstanding the lack of a Court and a
peerage, everybody did not go everywhere in America, and that social
exclusiveness and even social arro-

gance and the desire for social distinction and success were quite as great in America as in England, they looked at me and at each other with an expression of weak astonishment.

"Why," said Lady Boreham, " I thought you were democrats and communists and—and that sort of thing, and that you thought that nobody was any better than anybody else; although some of you, I believe, are awfully rich."

" Democracy, madam, in America is confined jealously to politics. As to wealth, money has rather more brute power in the United States, and particularly in New York, than it has in England,—where I believe it has not a little,—or in any other country in the world; and as to the effect of democracy upon society in America, it is briefly to beget a belief that on the one hand nobody is any better than you are, and on the other that very few are as good."

" Dear me,—dear me! Then you have exclusive circles in America too?"

" So exclusive that people may, and do in cases numberless, live in the same neighbourhood, and even next door to each other, for years, and never speak, and hardly know each other's names. So exclusive that often the richer of these neighbours would be very glad to obtain, by a considerable sacrifice, an entrance to the entertainments of the poorer."

" Dear, dear! Quite like w'at it is at 'ome; and I thought it was so different."

" Very like, indeed, so far as I may venture to have an opinion. For, strange to say, a democratic form of government has not yet produced in America any very great or manifest change in men as individuals. There still remains a great deal of human nature in the men and women there; nor does there yet appear much power in democracy to cast it out. As to the process called in both countries, I believe, getting into society, I have known a woman of great wealth, intelligence, and an untarnished reputation, push, and crawl, and bully, and flatter, spend money like water, be snubbed, and lie down and be trodden upon for years, to work her way into a certain set, and fail utterly."

"Dear, dear!" again bleated Lady Boreham from under the teeth; "just like it is at 'ome."

"And then this woman, having, by luck or contrivance, or both, obtained the notice and the favour of some distinguished person at home or abroad, was all at once taken up by society, and flaunted it grandly among the very people who a few years before treated her as if they were Brahmins and she a Pariah."

" Oh, *that's just* like it is at 'ome!" cried Maud, from the window. " For don't you remember, Charlotte, how that handsome Mrs."—

" Hush, Maud!" said Lady Boreham. "What *can* you know about it?"

" Yes, ' Hush, my dear, lie still and slumber,' " was heard from behind Sir Charles's *Times,* followed by a little rumble of laughter.

" Come," he said, seeing, I suspect, that I was a little weary of my society talk, " let's go to the stables, and I'll show you my dark bay, Tempest; the finest horse across country in——shire: takes anything I'll let him go at."

III.

Toppington Priory.
Lord Toppingham sees a "real American."

III.

TOPPINGTON PRIORY. LORD TOPPINGHAM SEES A "REAL AMERICAN."

HUMPHREYS was right. A day or two afterward, there came from the Priory an invitation to the Borehams to meet some people who were to be there at luncheon, in an informal way. "You'll go with us, of course," said Sir Charles. "We know the Toppinghams well, and they'll be very pleased to see you."

Indeed, the Borehams did know the Toppinghams well, and Borehams had known Toppinghams for generations. They had been neighbours and friends or neighbours and enemies, almost ever since England was England. They had fought Duke William at Hastings, and were among those who had been allowed to retain their little estates as vassals of one of the Conqueror's great barons. They fought together at Agincourt, each with his spear or two and his dozen or score of bowmen, under the banner of the lord of their marches. They had fought each other in the Wars of the Roses, when the Toppinghams were Lancastrians and the Borehams Yorkists. Together they had resisted the tyranny of Charles I., and had supported Sir William Waller—fondly called by the Parliament party William the Conqueror—in his triumphant march through the western counties; and together they had joined him in his defection from the Parliament, when it became revolutionary. There had been an intermarriage or two, in olden times; but of later years the Toppinghams had become ambitious in this respect, as well as in all others, while the Borehams went on their steady way, as simple English gentlemen. But such knowledge and friendship through centuries is full of meaning. There are no shams about it, or uncertainties or possible concealments.

The ladies and the M.P. drove over in a pony phaeton and a landau; but Sir Charles and I rode, he grumbling a little at losing a day's shooting. With our two grooms, we made a pretty little cavalcade on that bright, soft September morning; and we delighted in ourselves and in each other, as we trotted gently through the noble beauty of the grandly timbered park.

The Priory was a large, handsome, irregular stone pile, showing plainly its ecclesiastical origin; but it presented no remarkable features to distinguish it from many other great houses of its sort in England. Lord Toppingham received us in the hall with a bland but hearty welcome, in which there was a little spirit that was lacking even in Sir Charles's kindliness, when I arrived at Boreham; and his warm hand pressure and " So you've come at last," as he led us up the great staircase, made me feel that I had done well in accepting his double invitation. It also relieved me a little of my concern as to Humphreys' project, for I had not neglected to inform him of our proposed visit.

Our pleasure—mine, at least—was very much enhanced by our reception by Lady Toppingham, a fine elegant woman of about thirty years of age, very gentle of speech and gracious of manner, but with a manifest capacity of dash on good occasion. I suspect that she hunted; nor should I have objected to see that figure, lithe with all its largeness, in a riding habit, and on a worthy, well-groomed horse. A certain sense of spirit and force seemed to pervade the air at Toppingham, and to distinguish it from the sober, comfortable respectability of the house that we had left. I learned that Lady Toppingham's title, although not her coronet, was hers by birthright; she being the second daughter of the Marquis of A——. Her dress was in such perfect taste that it attracted no attention; we saw only her grace of movement and beauty of form.

Two or three guests were in the room with her when we entered; and out on the terrace, upon which a large window opened, were as many more, of whom hereafter. After salutation and a brief matter-of-course chat, we all went out upon the terrace to enjoy the air and the beauty of the park, stretching far away from the other side of a large old-fashioned garden, formally laid out, and planted with varied flowers in great masses of colour.

I could not but remark the bearing of Lady Boreham and her sister to Lady Toppingham. It might not, perhaps, be said that they cringed to her; but they fawned upon her, and " dear-Lady-Toppinghamed " her to herself and to each other in whirring adulation. Once, as I watched this toadying, I caught a light flash of scorn from her glancing eye, which made her beautiful. As to Sir Charles, he was as much at his unconscious ease as if he were a duke.

There were no introductions, and after a glance at my fellow-guests I attached myself to a young man of unmistakable soldierly bearing, who was standing apart in silence. He was a fine-looking fellow, with a simple and almost boyish face, whiskerless, but with a sweeping blonde moustache, to which from time to time he gave a pull; not foppish or military, but rather meditative. I liked these young English officers and their fellows, who, if not soldiers, were the stuff out of which soldiers are made; men who had been taught to ride, to shoot, and to speak the truth, and who, indeed, most of them, knew little else. Coming from New York, I found a sense of relief in their mere physical repose and manly steadiness. Their serenity seemed to me like that which looks at us out of the marble eyes of the old Greek statues.

I was reminded by it of a story told me in my youth by a friend of my father's age, who, sitting by an English lady of rank at a ball in New York, when he was a young man, saw that she was scrutinising with great interest the young people on the floor. He broke the silence by asking, "Well, what do you think of them? Not quite equal to your lads and lasses in England, are they?" "On the contrary," she replied, "I never saw finer young people in my life, nor better mannered. The girls are lovely; and as to the stories we've been told about their not having good figures, it's simply nonsense. But I wasn't thinking of the girls." "Well, the young men?" "They're fine fellows too, most of them, and well mannered; but, if you'll pardon me, as to their *manner* and their look"— "Well?" "Nothing, nothing; but they all look so sharp,—as if they had their eyes out on everybody else, and weren't quite sure of their surroundings. Now, with us, young fellows of their age and breeding wouldn't have the occasion to look sharp." The elderly friend who repeated to me this bit of social criticism, and who must have heard it quite fifty years ago, said that he could not but admit its justice in regard to the young New Yorkers. Were he living, what would he say now? Nevertheless, that there is in some of these young British lion-cubs stuff which the world's grindstone brings to a sharpness that puts to shame the craft of a Christian Greek or a Heathen Chinee, some of their American acquaintances have learned, to their sorrow.

My young friend on the terrace proved to be Captain the Honourable John Surcingle, of Her Majesty's 9th Dragoon Guards, second son of the Earl of Martingale, and my hostess's cousin. After a few words, I asked him to tell me the names of some of those around us, other than our own party.

"'Pon my life! can't say. Don't know where Toppin'em finds all his people. Toppin'em's vewy jolly; awfully nice fellow himself, you know; but"— Here he stopped, and, screwing his glass into his eye, looked quietly around for a few moments.

"Wather wum lot. Litwawy persons, or somethin', I sh'd say, most of 'em."

The captain's instincts had not misled him, as erelong I myself discovered. His "rum lot" included, among others who were literary, or something, Professor Schlamm, of the University of Bonn, who was on his first visit to England, to make arrangements for the publication, simultaneously, in English and German, of his profound work, in three volumes, 8vo, on *The Unity in Duality of the English Nation from the days of Hengist and Horsa to those of Victoria and Albert.* Then there was Lady Verifier, the young middle-aged widow of old Sir Duns Verifier, F.R.S.A., of the British Museum, who was knighted for having elaborated a stupendous plan of cataloguing the library of that institution, which upon trial proved so utterly impracticable and worthless that the old book-mole, smitten with shame and disappointment, went speedily to his grave; leaving his widow to enter literary life by publishing *Shadows of the Soul*, a poem in which art was shown to be " the plastic form of religion."

Of the others, there was now noteworthy only Mrs. Longmore, who was known as the authoress of *Immaculate*, a novel in which the somewhat startling experiences of the heroine were said by some people to be in a certain degree autobiographical.

Lady Verifier was spare, angular, and sallow, with large black eyes and coarse black hair, like a squaw's; a sort of woman less uncommon in England than she is supposed to be. Mrs. Longmore was her very opposite: fair, plump almost to portliness, with moist blue eyes and moist red lips.

There were one or two others of their sort; and the rest of our little company were unremarkable folk, of the Toppingham and Boreham class.

Erelong a servant entered, with a card upon a salver, which he presented to our hostess, who, after glancing at it a moment with a puzzled look, said, "To my Lord." On receiving it, his Lordship handed it to me, saying, "From your friend. He sent me a letter of introduction from Tooptoe at Oxford; said he couldn't come just now himself, and asked the favour of introducin', just for a mornin' visit, an American gentleman, in whom he felt sure I should be interested. It's all right, I suppose?" It was simply Humphreys' card, with a line in pencil, "introducing the Hon. Washington J. Adams."

"I don't know Mr. Adams," I said; "but I do know that Mansfield Humphreys would give a card to no one who might not be properly received by the gentleman to whom it was addressed."

Here Captain Surcingle, whose attention had been arrested, and who had heard my reply, cried out " 'Mewican? Have him up, Toppin'em,— have him up! Those fellows are such fun! I always go to see the 'Mewican Cousin. Not faw Dundweawy. Can't see what they make such a doosid fuss about him faw. Does nothin' but talk just like ' fellow at the Wag: wegla' muff. Nevah saw such a boa. But Twenchard's awful fun ; good as goin' to 'Mewica without the boa of goin'."

As the Honourable John began his appeal, his lady cousin stepped across the terrace to pluck a rose which peered at us over the stone balustrade, blushing with shame at its beautiful intrusion ; and as she swept past him, I partly heard and partly saw her say, in an earnest whisper, "Jack, *do* be quiet; and *don't* be such a goose!"

As she turned back with her flower, the servant who had been sent out returned, and announced "Mr. Adams;" and all eyes followed our host, as he stepped forward to receive him. As unabashed as a comet intruding upon the solar system, the Honourable Washington stepped into our circle, and met its sun and his satellites. The Earl offered him his hand. He took it, and then he shook it,—shook it well; and to a few of the usual words of welcome he replied, "I'm very glad to see you, my Lord; most happy to hev the pleasure of meetin' your Lordship" (looking round) "here in your elegant doughmain and your gorjis castle. My friend Mr. Humphreys told me I'd find everything here fuss class; an' I hev. Your man help downstairs wuz a leetle slow, to be sure; but don't apologise; difference of institootions, I s'pose. Everything moves a leetle slower here."

As Lord Toppingham led Mr. Adams to our hostess, eyes of wonder, not unmixed with pleasure, were bent upon him. He was a man of middle size, neither tall nor slender; but he stooped a little from his hips, and his head was slightly thrust forward, with an expression of eagerness, as he slouched along the terrace. His upper lip was shaved; but his sallow face terminated in that adornment known at the West as "chin-whiskers." His hat, which he kept on, was of felt, with a slightly conical crown. It rested rather on the back than on the top of his head, and from it fell a quantity of longish straight brown hair. His splendid satin scarf was decorated with a large pin, worthy of its position; and the watch-chain that stretched across his waistcoat would

H

have held a yacht to its moorings. His outer garment left the beholder in doubt whether it was an overcoat that he was wearing as a duster, or a duster doing service as an overcoat. Into the pockets of this he thrust his hands deep, and moved them back and forth from time to time, giving the skirts a wing-like action. Having taken Lady Toppingham's hand, and shaken that too, and assured her of his pleasure in meeting her also, he put his own back into its appropriate pocket, and gently flapping his wings, repeated, " Yes, ma'am; very happy to hev the pleasure of meetin' your Ladyship. Hope my call ain't put you out any; but I s'pose you're used to seein' a goodle o' company in the surprise way."

" I am always pleased to receive any friend of my Lord's or of Dr. Tooptoe's," said Lady Toppingham, seating herself upon one of the stone benches of the terrace; and Lord Toppingham turned as if to lead Mr. Adams away. But that gentleman immediately sat himself down by her side, and, crossing his legs, was evidently preparing to make himself agreeable. A slight shade of reserve with which she had taken her seat deepened for a moment, and then instantly gave way to a look of good-natured amusement; and I saw, to my relief, that she appreciated the situation. "You've been in our little England before, I suppose, Mr. Adams?"

"No, ma'am, I hevn't. My plit'cle dooties as a member of the legislater of the Empire State hev pervented. Empire State's Noo York, 'z I s'pose your Ladyship knows. Motto, Excelsior, an' the risin' sun; out of Longfeller's poem, you know."

"I do know Mr. Longfellow's charming poem. We're great admirers of

Mr. Longfellow in England; indeed, we think him quite an English poet."

" Wal, ma'am, you're 'baout right there; 'xcept in callin' him an English poet. He's a true Muh'kin; an' he kin beat Tennyson, an' all the rest of 'em, at writin' poetry, any day, let 'em do their level best. Why, he's written more vollums of poetry—fuss-class poetry, too—than any man that ever lived; more'n Dr. Holland. Lives in fuss-class style, too, if he is a poet. Shouldn't wonder if there wa'nt a broker in Wall Street that lives in higher style than Longfeller."

At this triumphant utterance Mr. Adams took off his hat, and I feared he was about to wave it; but the movement was only one of momentary relief to his enthusiasm, and he at once restored it to its perilous inclination.

Lord Toppingham now stepped up to create a diversion in favour of his beleaguered wife, and, standing before the pair, asked Mr. Adams if he had been in London while Parliament was sitting.

"Wal, yaas, I wuz," replied the legislator, keeping his seat and looking up; " 'n' I went to see it; 'n' to tell the truth 'n' the hull truth, I wuz dis'pinted. Gladstone's a smart man, but slow, I shed say,—mighty slow; ain't learned not to craowd himself, nuther; bites off more 'n he kin chaw. 'N' I didn't hear no elo-quence; nobody didn't seem to take no intrust into what was goin' on. You hev got a powerful han'some buildin' fur the meetin' of your legislater; but jess you wait 'n' see the noo Capitol 't Albany, 'n' you 'll sing small, I—tell —you. Yes, siree."

As this conversation went on, some of the other guests had approached, and there was a little group around our hostess and Mr. Adams, who now, to the evident horror of some of them, drew from his pocket a gigantic knife, with a set-spring at the back; indeed, it was a clasp bowie-knife. Opening it with a tremendous click, he strapped it a little on his shoe, and then looked doubtfully at the bench on which he sat. Evidently dissatisfied with the inducement which its stone surface offered, he drew from one of his capacious pockets a piece of pine wood about as thick as a heavy broomstick, and began to cut it in a meditative manner.

"Don't git much whittlin' into your effete old monarchies. Even the benches, when they ain't stun, air oak, that 'd turn the edge of any gen'leman's knife; 'n' so I carry suthin' comfortable raound with me;" and as he spoke the light shavings curled away from his stick, and rolled upon the terrace floor.

Lady Toppingham was as serene as

a harvest moon, and was evidently much amused with her visitor; and the rest looked on with an interest and a satisfaction which were manifest in their countenances.

"Your Lordship does suthin' in this way, I reckon. Guess all you lords are in the lumber line; 'n' I seen some fuss-class trees inter the vacant lots round your haouse—castle, I mean. S'pose that's the reason you don't improve. Much doin' in lumber naow?"

"Not much," said our host, with a pleasant smile. "I'm more inclined to keep my trees than to sell them, at present. But let me make you acquainted with some of my friends. Mr. Grimstone, member for Hilchester Towers."

"Haow do you do, Mr. Grimstone?" said Adams, rising; and shifting his knife to his left hand, he took the M.P.'s, and shaking it vigorously, said,

"Happy to hev the pleasure of meetin' you, sir. Don't know you personally, but know you very well by reputtation."

As our host looked next at me, I managed to convey to him an unspoken request not to be introduced, which he respected; but my friend the captain, stepping forward, was presented, with the added comment that Mr. Adams would find him well up about guns and rifles and fire-arms of all kinds; quite an authority, indeed, upon that subject.

"Dew tell? Why, I'm glad to hev the pleasure of meetin' you, sir. Look a' here! I kin show you suthin' fuss class in that line;" and putting his hand behind him, underneath his coat, he produced a large pistol, a navy revolver, which he exhibited in a demonstrative way to the captain, saying, "Naow that's suthin' satisfactory fur a gen'leman to hev about him; no little pea-shootin' thing, that you might empty into a man 'thout troublin' him more 'n so many flea-bites."

The captain looked at it with interest, while some of the other guests shrank away. After a brief examination, he returned it, saying, "Vewy fine, vewy fine indeed; and I hear you use 'em at vewy long distances, almost like a wifle."

"Sartin," said Mr. Adams. "Look a' here! See that thar tree yonder?" and pointing to one on the other side of the garden, he threw up his left arm, and took a sight rest on it. Some of the ladies screamed, and the captain and Lord Toppingham both caught his arm, the latter exclaiming, "Beg pahdon, don't fire, please! Somebody might be passin' in the park."

"Wal, jess's *you* like, sir. You air to hum, en I ain't. But that's the diff'kilty 'ith England. Th'r'ain't no libbuty here. You 've allers got to be thinkin' 'baout somebody else."

The incident certainly created a little unpleasant excitement; yet after this had subsided, it seemed not to have diminished, but rather to have increased, the satisfaction with which Mr. Adams was regarded. The Professor came up, and said, "Our Amerigan vrent is ferry kint sooch an exhipition of the manners and gustoms of his gountry to gif. Barehaps he vould a var-tance bareform vor the inztrugzion oond blaysure off dthe gompany."

"No, no, Professor Schlamm," said Lady Toppingham, smiling, "we won't put Mr. Adams to the trouble of a war-dance; and we 've so narrowly escaped one *blessure* that we may well be willing to forego the other." As my hostess struck off this little spark, I observed that her French was not that of the school of Stratford atte

Bowe, which continues much in vogue in England even among ladies of the prioress's rank.

Adams caught at the name as an introduction. "Is this," he said, "the celebrated Professor Schlamm?" and seizing his hand, he shook it well. "Happy to make your acquaintance, sir. Your fame, sir, is widely extended over the civilised globe. Hevn't hed the pleasure of meetin' you before, sir, but know you very well by reputtation."

The Professor, who had all the simple vanity of the vainest race in the world, beamed under the influence of this compliment, so that his very spectacles seemed to glow with warmth and light.

"You German gen'l'men air fond of our naytional plant," said Adams blandly. "Hev a cigar? Won't you jine me?" and he produced from his pocket two or three temptations.

" Dthanks; poot it might not to dthe laties pe acreeaple."

" No ? Wal, then, here goes fur the ginooine article. I 'm 'baout tuckered aout fur some." Saying this, he took from another pocket a brown plug, cut off a piece, and, having shaped and smoothed it a little with his huge knife, he laid it carefully with his forefinger in his cheek. Then, his knife being out, he took the opportunity to clean his nails; and having scraped the edges until our blood curdled, he returned his weapon, after a loud click, to his pocket.

A look of distress had come over the face of our hostess when Mr. Adams produced his plug; and she called a servant, who, after receiving an order from her in a low voice, went out. Mr. Adams's supplementary toilet being completed, he slouched away towards the balustrade; and after looking a few moments across the garden, he turned about, and, leaning against the stone, he began an expectorative demonstration. After he had made two or three violent and very obtrusive efforts of this kind, which, however, I must confess, did not seem to leave much visible witness before us, the servant returned hastily with a spittoon, the fabric and condition of which showed very plainly that it came from no part of the Priory that rejoiced in the presence of Lady Toppingham. This the footman placed before Mr. Adams, within easy range.

"Nev' mind," said that gentleman, —"nev' mind. Sorry you took the trouble, sonny. I don't set up fur style; don't travel onto it. I'm puffickly willin' to sit down along 'th my fren's, and spit round sociable. I know I wear a biled shirt 'n' store clothes,—that's a fact; but's a graceful con-ciliation *of* and deference *to* public opinion, considerin' I'm a member of the legislater of the Empire State."

" Biled ? " said Captain Surcingle to me, inquiringly (for we had kept pretty close together). " Mean boiled ? "

" Yes."

" Boil shirts in 'Mewica ? "

" Always."

" Your shirt boiled ? "

" N-no ; not exactly. I should have said that all our wealthiest and most distinguished citizens, members of the legislature and the like, boil their shirts. I make no such pretensions."

The captain looked at me doubtfully. But our talk and Mr. Adams's performances were brought to a close by the announcement of luncheon, and an invitation from our host to the dining-room. This midday repast is quite informal ; but, comparatively unrestrained as it is by etiquette, rank and precedence are never quite forgotten at it, or on any other occasion, in England; and there being no man of rank present, except our host, and Sir Charles being far down the terrace, talking hunt and horse with another squire, Mr. Grimstone was moving toward Lady Toppingham, with the expectation of entering with her, when Mr. Adams stepped quickly up, and saying, "Wal, I don't keer ef I dew jine you; 'low me the pleasure, ma'am," he offered her his arm. She took it. Mr. Grimstone retreated in disorder, and we all went in somewhat irregularly. As we passed through the hall, and approached the dining-room, it occurred to Mr. Adams to remove his hat; and he then looked about, and up and down, in evident search of a peg on which to hang it. A servant stepped forward, and held out his hand for it. After a brief hesitation he resigned it, saying, "Ain't ye goin' to give me no check for that? Haow do I know I'll git it agin? Haowever, it's Lord Toppingham's haouse, an' he's responsible, I guess. That's good law, ain't it, your Lordship?"

"Excellent," said our host, evidently much pleased that Lady Toppingham had taken this opportunity to continue on her way to the dining-room, where we found her with Mr. Grimstone on her right hand, and a vacant seat on her left, between her and her cousin, to which she beckoned me; Mr. Adams, the Professor, and the two authoresses forming a little group near Lord Toppingham.

"I hope," said the M.P. to me, as we were settling ourselves at table, "that you are pleased with your Mr. Washington Adams. I, for one, own that such a characteristic exhibition of genuine American character and manners is, if not exactly agreeable, a very entertaining subject of study."

The taunt itself was less annoying than its being flung at me across our hostess; but as I could not tell him so without sharing his breach of good manners, I was about to let his remark pass, with a silent bow, when a little look of encouragement in Lady Toppingham's eyes led me to say, "As to your entertainment, sir, I have no doubt that you might find as good at home without importing your Helots. As to Mr. Adams being my Mr. Washington Adams, he is neither kith nor kin of any of my people, to whom he would be an occasion of as much curious wonder as he is to any person at this table."

"Oh, that won't do at all. He is one of your legislators,—the Honourable Washington Adams. You Americans are a very strange people; quite incomprehensible to our poor, simple English understandings." I did not continue the discussion, which

I saw would be as fruitless as, under the circumstances, it was unpleasant, and indeed almost inadmissible, notwithstanding the gracious waiver of my hostess.

Luncheon engaged the attention of us all for a while, notwithstanding the presence of Mr. Adams; but nevertheless he continued to be the chief object of attention; and erelong he was heard saying, with an elevated voice, in evident continuation of description of a legislative scene, " The feller, sir, had the lip to perpose to investigate me; but I told him, sir, that I courted investigation, and I claimed that he was no better than a scallawag and a shyster: and I gripped him, sir, and skun him,—skun him clean as an eel."

Captain Surcingle, who had been regarding the speaker with all the earnestness that his glass admitted, turned to me, and said, with soft inquiry—

"Skun? 'Mewican for skinned?"

"Yes; all true Americans say skun."

"Vewy queeah way of speakin' English;" and he was about to subside into silence, when all at once a bright gleam of intelligence came into his face, and he broke out, "Oh, I say! that won't do. You're 'Mewican; an' you don't say skun or scallawag;" and the good fellow regarded me with a look of triumph.

"Yes," I replied; "but you see I'm not a full-blooded American, as Mr. Adams is,—only a Yankee. Then I've had some special advantages. I've been in Canada; and that is still one of the British possessions. Besides, I'm fond of reading; and friends in England have sent me a few London books,—books with 'honor' spelled with a *u*, and all that sort of thing. Don't you see?"

"Ah, yes. Just so, just so; quite so." And now he was silent. But candour compels me to admit that he did not seem to be quite satisfied, and that, as he slowly ate jugged hare, he appeared to be wrestling with some intellectual problem that was too much for him.

Here the butler asked Mr. Adams if he should not change his plate. "Wal, yes, sir, ef you'd like to. I'm sure I've no 'bjecshin." Another plate was placed before him, and he was asked what he would have. "Wal, I guess I'll take a leetle more o' th' same,—that thar pie thar, 'ith the chicken fixins into it," pointing with a wave of his knife at a pheasant pie, of which he had just eaten. "I call that fuss class, I do. Does you credit, ma'am," he said blandly, addressing the Countess,—"does you credit. I must get you to give me the receipt for Mrs. Adams. You air slow here, an' a goodle behind the lighter; but 'baout eatin' and drinkin' you air pooty smart, I calklate."

Here Lord Toppingham, probably to divert attention from Mr. Adams, looking across the table at me, expressed his surprise that so little had been produced in American literature and art that was peculiarly American; that all our best writers wrote merely as Englishmen would, treating the same subjects; and that our painters and sculptors seemed to form their styles upon those of Italy and Greece.

"Yes, indeed," said Lady Verifier. "Where is that effluence of the newborn individual soul that should emanate from a fresh and independent democracy, the possessors of a continent, with a Niagara and a Mississippi between two vast oceans? You profess to be a great people, but you have evolved no literature, no art of your own. You see the sun rise from the Atlantic, and set in the Pacific;

and it seems to do you no good, but to send you to Europe for your language and to Japan for your decoration."

"Lady Ferifier is fery right," said Professor Schlamm. "Ameriga is a gountry of brovound dizabbointment to dthe vilozovig mind. It is pig oond rich; poot noding orichinal toes it brotuce."

"Nothing that springs from the soil and savours of the soil," said Lady Verifier.

"Except its Washington Adamses," said the M.P., in a surly undertone.

"My Lord," I answered, "your question and Lady Verifier's remind me of a paragraph that I saw quoted from a London sporting paper, a short time ago, about American horses." (Here Captain Surcingle dropped his knife and fork, and turned his glass on me.) "It accounted for the fact that American horses had won so many cups lately by the other fact that the Americans had been importing English horses, and thus had improved their stock; so that in truth the cups had been won by England, after all."

"That's jolly good," said the captain.

"Now that is quite true. But it is only half the truth; for the whole truth is that all our horses are English. The horse is not indigenous to America. Neither are we. We are not autochthones, as by your expectations it would seem you think us. We are not products of the soil. We are not the fruit of Niagara or the prairies, which most of us have never been within five hundred miles of; nor of the oceans, which few of us have ever seen. We are what we are by race and circumstances; not because we live on a certain part of the earth's surface. If you want a literature and an art that smack of the soil, you must go to Sitting Bull and Squatting Bear, with whom we have no other relations than we, or you, have with the cave-dwellers. Nor do Americans live and manage their affairs with the purpose of satisfying the philosophic mind, of working out interesting social problems, or of creating a new literature and a new art, but simply to get, each one of them, as much material comfort out of life and the world as to him is possible ; a not very novel notion in the human creature."

"And so, sir," said Mr. Adams, speaking to me for the first time, in tones which, when addressed to me, seemed to have something familiar in them, " that is your patriotic veoo of your country? And may I ask what good thing you think is peculiar to 'Muh'ky?"

" Food for the hungry and freedom for the oppressed.'

"Nothing else?" asked our host.

"Nothing."

"But to the wide benevolence of an American democrat I suppose that is enough," said Lady Toppingham.

"Pardon me, madam, but I sometimes think that birth and breeding in a democratic country may make men aristocrats of the blackest dye; and I go about fancying that some of us ought to have been guillotined forty or fifty years before we were born, as enemies to the human race."

"Oh, I say," cried the captain, "that won't do! Couldn't guillotine 'fellah b'foah he was bawn, you know."

"Nevertheless, my dear captain, I'm inclined to believe that it might better have been done."

"Vewy stwange," drawled the Honourable John.

Here Mr. Adams, as he was regarding me with fixed and desperate eye, drew his bowie-knife from his pocket and opened it ; but before the horror of an expected onslaught upon me could well have thrilled the company, he quieted all apprehensions, if not all nerves, by picking his teeth with it in a very deliberate manner.

Meantime the two authoresses and the Professor were talking with animation; and I heard fragmentarily, "dear Walt Whitman," " most enthralling of American writers," " egsbrezzion of dthe droo Amerigan sbirit ;" and Lord Toppingham, looking at our end of the table, said, " Our literary friends here insist that you *have* one truly representative author; one who represents, not perhaps your cultured classes, but the feelin's and hopes and aspirations of those people who are the true representatives of the American genius."

" Yaas," said Mr. Adams.

" As to that, I can only refer you to Mr. Stedman, a writer whom some of your Victorian Poets ought to know; and who has seen and recorded the fact that Walt Whitman is entirely disregarded, and almost contemned, by our people of the plainer and humbler sort, who find in him no expression of their feelings or their thoughts; and that he is considered (for I cannot say that he is read) only by the curious, the critical, the theorists, and the dilettanti,—the fastidious aristocracy and literary *bric-à-brac* hunters of the intellectual world. As to his poetry, except on some rare occasions when he lapses into common-sense and human feeling, it is simply naught. Erelong some of you in England will be ashamed of the attention you have given to its affectations. The merit that it has you would have passed over without notice. It is written in a jargon unknown to us. The very title of his book is in a language that I never heard spoken."

"What can you mean?"

"I was brought up in New England and New York, and never there, nor yet in Old England, nor in any of the literature common to both countries, did I hear of 'leaves of grass.' Grass has not what in English we call leaves. We have blades of grass, even spears; but who ever heard of leaves? A trifle this; but coming on the title-page, it proves to be a sign of what's within."

"My very paytriotic friend," said Mr. Adams sarcastically, "thet's a sort of 'bjecshin thet ud do fur th' *Sahturday Reveoo;* but 't won't go daown 'th any true 'Muh'kin. Ef 'Muh'ky wants leaves o' grass 'nstid o' blades, she'll hev 'em. I kin put all that daown jess by readin' a piece thet I've got into my pocket,—one thet Walt Whitman's never published yet; but I kerry it raound to read sorter b'tween whiles."

The reading was loudly called for, and Mr. Adams, producing a sheet or two of paper from his all-containing pocket, read as follows :—

1 I happify myself.
   I am considerable of a man. I am some. You also are some. We all are considerable; all are some.
   Put all of you and all of me together, and agitate our particles by rubbing us up into eternal smash, and we should still be some.
   No more than some, but no less.
   Particularly some, some particularly; some in general, generally some; but always some, without mitigation. Distinctly, some!
   O ensemble! O quelque-chose!

2 Some punkins, perhaps;
   But perhaps squash,[1] long-necked squash, crooked-necked squash, cucumber, beets, parsnips, carrots, turnips, white turnips, yellow turnips, or any sort of sass; long sass or short sass.
   Or potatoes. Men, Irish potatoes; women, sweet potatoes.

---

[1] Squash is an American vegetable like a very small pumpkin, tasting like vegetable marrow.

3 Yes, women!
I expatiate myself in female man.
A reciprocity treaty. Not like a jug's handle.
They look at me, and my eyes start out of my head; they speak to me, and I yell with delight; they shake hands with me, and things are mixed; I don't know exactly whether I 'm them; or them 's me.
Women watch for me; they do. Yes, sir!
They rush upon me; seven women laying hold of one man; and the divine efflux that thrilled the cosmos before the nuptials of the saurians overflows, surrounds, and interpenetrates their souls, and they cry, Where is Walt, our brother? Why does he tarry, leaving us forlorn?
O, mes sœurs!

As Mr. Adams read this in a voice heavily monotonous and slightly nasal, the whole company listened with animation in their faces. Lord Toppingham looked puzzled. Lady Toppingham smiled, a little cynically, I thought. The M.P. sat with open, wondering eyes. Professor Schlamm, at the conclusion of the first stanza, folded his hands upon the table, putting his two thumbs together, and leaning forward looked through his spectacles at the reader with solemnity. Lady Verifier exclaimed, "A truly cyclical utterance; worthy to be echoed through the eternal æons!" Mrs. Longmore, at the end of the third stanza, murmured, "Divine! divine! America is the new Paradise." Captain Surcingle turned to me, and asked, "What language is it witten in,—'Mewican?"

Then Mr. Adams continued:—

57 Of Beauty.
  Of excellence, of purity, of honesty, of truth.
  Of the beauty of flat-nosed, pock-marked, pied Congo niggers.
  Of the purity of compost-heaps, the perfume of bone-boiling; of the fragrance of pig-sties, and the ineffable sweetness of general corruption.
  Of the honesty and general incorruptibility of political bosses, of aldermen, of common-council men, of postmasters and

government contractors, of members of the House of Representatives, and of government officers generally, of executors of wills, of trustees of estates, of referees, and of cashiers of banks who are Sunday-school superintendents. Of the truth of theatrical advertisements, and advertisements generally, of an actor's speech on his benefit night, of your salutation when you say, "I am happy to see you, sir," of Mrs. Lydia Pinkham's public confidences, of the miracles worked by St. Jacob's Oil, and the long-recorded virtues of Scheidam schnapps.

58 I glorify schnapps; I celebrate gin.
In beer I revel and welter. I shall liquor.
Ein lager!
I swear there is no nectar like lager. I swim in it; I float upon it; it heaves me up to heaven; it bears me beyond the stars; I tread upon the ether; I spread myself abroad; I stand self-poised in illimitable space. I look down; I see you; I am no better than you. You also shall mount with me.
Zwei lager!
Encore.

1003 O, my soul!
O, your soul! which is no better than my soul, and no worse, but just the same.
O soul in general! Loafe! Proceed through space with rent garments.
O shirt out-issuing, pendent! O tattered, fluttering flag of freedom! Not national freedom, nor any of that sort of infernal nonsense; but freedom individual, freedom to do just what you d— [here Mr. Adams gulped the word] please!

1004 By golly, there is nothing in this world so unutterably magnificent as the inexplicable comprehensibility of inexplicableness!

1005 Of mud.

1006 O eternal circles, O squares, O triangles, O hypotenuses, O centres, circumferences, diameters, radiuses, arcs, sines, co-sines, tangents, parallelograms and parallelopipedons! O pipes that are not parallel, furnace pipes, sewer pipes, meerschaum pipes, brier-wood pipes, clay pipes! O matches, O fire, and coal-scuttle, and shovel, and tongs, and fender, and ashes, and dust, and dirt! O everything! O nothing! O myself! O yourself! O my eye!

At this point of the reading the enthusiastic admiration of some of the audience again broke silence. "That noble passage," cried Lady Verifier, "beginning with the eternal circles, and ending with everything and nothing! So vast! so all-inspiring!"

"So all-embracing!" sighed Mrs. Longmore.

"Zo univarezall," said the Professor, "zo voondamentahl, zo brovound! Go on, my vrent, oond de zing-zong shant, und de evangel bredigate, of the noo vorlt; oond I zoon a vilozophy of dthe Amerigan zoul zhall write."

Mr. Adams resumed:—

1247 These things are not in Webster's
    Dictionary, Unabridged Pictorial;
  Nor yet in Worcester's. Wait and get
    the best.

These have come up out of the ages:
Out of the ground that you crush with your boot-heel:
Out of the muck that you have shovelled away into the compost:
Out of the offal that the slow, lumbering cart, blood-dabbled and grease-dropping, bears away from the slaughter-house, a white-armed boy sitting on top of it, shouting Hi! and licking the horse on the raw, with the bridle.
That muck has been many philosophers; that offal was once gods and sages.
And I verify that I don't see why a man in gold spectacles and a white cravat, stuck up in a library, stuck up in a pulpit, stuck up in a professor's chair, stuck up in a governor's chair or in a president's chair, should be of any more account than a possum or a wood-chuck.
Libertad, and the divine average!

1249 I tell you the truth. Salut!
I am not to be bluffed off. No, sir!
I am large, hairy, earthy, smell of the soil, am big in the shoulders, narrow in the flank, strong in the knees, and of an inquiring and communicative disposition.

Also instructive in my propensities ; given to contemplation ; and able to lift anything that is not too heavy.
Listen to me, and I will do you good.
Loafe with me, and I will do you better.
And if any man gets ahead of me, he will find me after him.
Vale![1]

There was a hum of admiration around Mr. Adams as he restored the manuscript to his pocket; but Captain Surcingle turned to me, and asked, " 'Mewican poetwy?"

"Yes, Jack," said his cousin, answering for me; "and some of our wise people say that it's the only poetry that can be called American; but if it is, I am content with my English Longfellow."

"And I, madam, with my still more English Whittier."

[1] Readers of *The New York Albion* in 1860 may have memories awakened by these lines, but I am able to ensure Mr. Adams against a suit for copyright, or a charge of plagiarism.

This Mr. Adams evidently thought would be a good opportunity to bring his visit to an end, and rising in his place, with a manner as if addressing the chair, he said, "My Lord, I shall now bid your Lordship farwell; an' in doin' so I thank you for your elegint en' bountiful hospitality. It wuz fuss class, en' thar wuz plenty of it; en' I shall remember it 'z long 'z I live. En' I thank your good lady, too, en' feel specially obleeged to her Ladyship fur that thar pie 'i' the chicken-fixin's into it. It *wuz* fuss class, and no mistake. En' now I hope you 'll all jine me in drinkin' her Ladyship's health; en' long may she wave. I can't call for the hips and the tiger, seein' there 's so many ladies present; but let's all liquor up, and knock down, and no heel-taps."

"Weal 'Mewican," said the captain, with an air of satisfaction. "Know it now. Wasn't quite sure befoah; but when he said liquor up 'knew he was weal."

The company had risen, and had drunk Mr. Adams's toast, and now broke up. He took, I thought, a rather hurried leave. The fourwheeled cab in which he came had remained, and was at the door, to which some of us accompanied him. When he was seated he looked out, and said, "If your Lordship ever comes to New York, jess look inter my office. Happy to see you. Name's into the D'rect'ry. So long!"

As the cab turned down the drive, we saw Mr. Adams's boot thrust itself lazily out of one of the windows, and rest there at its ease.

"First time 'ever saw 'weal 'Mewican off the stage," said the captain, slipping his arm into mine as we entered the hall again. "Vewy intwestin'. Think I shouldn't like it as a wegula' thing, you know."

Since my return to New York, I have inquired in vain for Mr. Washington Adams. Many persons seem to recognise my description of him as that of a man they have seen, but no one knows him by name; nor is there any such member of the New York legislature. I have not yet been able to ask Humphreys to resolve my perplexity.

THE END.

Edinburgh University Press:
T. AND A. CONSTABLE, PRINTERS TO HER MAJESTY.

www.ingramcontent.com/pod-product-compliance
Lightning Source LLC
Chambersburg PA
CBHW030317170426
43202CB00009B/1036